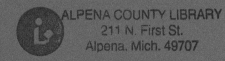

I Am Christmas

WRITTEN BY *Nancy White Carlstrom*

ILLUSTRATED BY *Lori McElrath-Eslick*

WILLIAM B. EERDMANS PUBLISHING COMPANY   •   GRAND RAPIDS, MICHIGAN

© 1995 Wm. B. Eerdmans Publishing Co.

255 Jefferson Ave. S.E., Grand Rapids, Michigan 49503

All rights reserved

Printed in Hong Kong

00 99 98 97 96   7 6 5 4 3 2

Library of Congress Cataloging-in-Publication Data

Carlstrom, Nancy White.
  I am Christmas / by Nancy White Carlstrom;
illustrated by Lori McElrath-Eslick.
      p.   cm.
  ISBN 0-8028-5075-8
    1. Jesus Christ — Nativity — Juvenile literature.
2. Christmas — Juvenile literature.
[1. Jesus Christ — Nativity. 2. Christmas.]
I. McElrath-Eslick, Lori, ill.   II. Title.
BT315.2C365   1995
232.92 — dc20   94-47931
                        CIP

Book design by Joy Chu

*For Marilyn E. Marlow,
with love —*N. W. C.

*To Mark and Sheila,
in God's grace and love —*L. M. E.

I am the way
they walk—these people,
who pass
up hill and down
going to the town
to be counted.

I am the vine

fruitful with branches

growing entwined

by the side of the road

as they walk this way

up hill and down

going to the town

to be counted.

I am the cup

purple with drink,

made from the grapes

of the vine,

branches entwined

by the side of the road.

I am the bread

baked in the oven,

packed for the journey,

broken and shared with others

together with stories and songs

as they walk this way

up hill and down

going to the town

to be counted.

I am the lily

she wears in her hair,

the rose

that blooms on her gown.

I am the news

he carries that came

in the angel dream

with the name

Emmanuel,

"God with us."

I am the light

they lift in the night

that brightens the darkness

as they walk this way

up hill and down

going to the town

to be counted.

I am the shepherd

who stands in the field,

the door to the fold

where I call my sheep:

"Come out of the cold

and be warm"—

as they walk this way

up hill and down

going to the town

to be counted.

I am the truth

they find when they seek

as they walk through the town

up roads and down —

many are here to be counted.

I am the life

breathed into this place,

no matter how lowly,

in time and in space

I am born.

Wrapped in a baby,

heralded by angels,

Lion and Lamb made holy.

I am the bright morning star

that fills the night

with a voice so big

and a light as high as the heavens

spilling to earth.

They hear. They see. They come.

I am the Word

he keeps in his sight

she keeps in her heart

they hear in the night

on hillsides of country,

in houses of town.

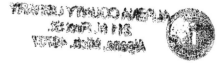

I am the gift

God gives to his children

sent down from above

to the world.

I AM CHRISTMAS

I am beginning, I am end,

the message foretold

scratched in sand

etched in gold—

I am the story, I am the song.

Scripture References for Symbols and Names of Christ

Way	John 14:6
Vine	John 15:1-5
Cup	Mark 14:23-24
Bread	John 6:35
Lily, Rose of Sharon	Song of Solomon 2:1
Emmanuel	Matthew 1:23
Light	John 1:5
Shepherd	John 10:11
Door	John 10:9
Truth	John 14:6
Life	John 1:4
Bright Morning Star	Revelation 22:16
Word	John 1:14
Gift	John 3:16

NANCY WHITE CARLSTROM *is the author of more than thirty books for children, including* Does God Know How to Tie Shoes?, Goodbye Geese, *and* Northern Lullaby. *She lives in Fairbanks, Alaska, with her husband and two sons.*

LORI McELRATH-ESLICK *is a freelance illustrator whose work appears regularly in* Ladybug *magazine. She has illustrated three picture books for children, including* Does God Know How to Tie Shoes? *She lives in North Muskegon, Michigan, with her husband and daughter.*